ANIMAL LIVES

The Otter

KINGFISHER
Kingfisher Publications Plc
New Penderel House, 283–288 High Holborn,
London WC1V 7HZ

First published in hardback by Kingfisher Publications Plc 1999
2 4 6 8 10 9 7 5 3 1

1(TR)/0299/SC/RPR(NEW)/150NYM

First published in paperback by Kingfisher Publications Plc 2000
2 4 6 8 10 9 7 5 3

2(TR)/0400/SC/RPR(NEW)/150NYM

A CIP catalogue record for this book is available
from the British Library.

ISBN 0 7534 0316 1 (hb)
ISBN 0 7534 0461 3 (pb)

Series editor: Miranda Smith
Series designer: Sarah Goodwin

Printed in Hong Kong / China

ANIMAL LIVES
The Otter

Illustrated by
Bert Kitchen

Written by
Sandy Ransford

KINGFISHER

As the shadows lengthen and the day draws to its close, a sleek brown animal slips silently from its hole in the river bank. The otter is off to hunt for food. Taking a deep breath, and closing her ears and nostrils to keep out the water, she dives. Powerful web-footed hind legs propel her swiftly forward; her strong, thick tail steers. She stays under for about half a minute, then comes up to breathe.

Fast as an arrow, slippery as an eel, the otter shoots through the water, twisting and turning after her prey. Although hunting is a serious business, she seems to swim for sheer joy. Fish, eels, frogs, voles – even ducklings and coots – make up her supper. Her speed lets her sneak up on them without warning. She eats smaller creatures under water, but carries larger ones to the shore.

So lithe and graceful in the water, the otter moves clumsily on land. With her long body arching upwards she waddles like a duck, dragging her tail along the ground. She shakes the water out of her coat; tiny droplets sparkle in the moonlight. Then she settles down to eat a favourite food, a large eel. Because it is slippery, she holds it between her forepaws as she chews. After her meal, she will groom herself, like a cat. Grooming spreads oil from her skin along the hairs, to help keep her coat waterproof.

Whether on land or in the water, the otter is always on the lookout for danger. People and dogs are especially threatening. At the slightest hint of someone approaching – the snap of a brittle twig, rustling in the grass – she will slip silently into the water, bolt for her hole, or, if it is too far away, hide in the nearest undergrowth. She has caught a strange scent in the air so, to get a good look, she rears up, propping herself with her tail. But this time it is not danger that approaches, but another otter. It is a young male, seeking a mate. For most of the year otters live alone. But the droppings and scent they leave behind act as messages to other otters. A female otter's droppings can tell a male that she is ready to breed. When he detects this, he will track her down.

The two otters meet, then tumble together into the water and start to play, chasing fish and ducks and each other, diving and somersaulting, twisting and turning, spiralling round and round each other in delight. They will romp together like this for several hours, playing both in and out of the water. It is their way of getting to know each other, so they can become friends.

They leap from the water and bound along the river bank, chasing each other and playing tag. The female stops for a moment to shake droplets of glistening river water out of her coat; the male joins her, then the two otters roll on the grass to dry themselves. Their thick, wet fur reflects the light, helping them to take on the appearance of their surroundings, and making them difficult to spot. But they only pause for a few moments before resuming their play, racing up and down, pouncing on each other and rolling over, then rushing off again. Eventually, when they have got to know each other really well, the two otters will become mates. The female signals to the male that she is ready to accept him as a mate by rolling over on her back with her paws in the air.

At dawn, the female otter is swimming home. Her holt might be a hole in a river bank, or between rocks on a quiet coastline. It has two entrances, one under water, so she can come and go without being seen. For most of the year she lives alone, travelling each night in search of food, sleeping each day in a different holt. Even though she now has a mate, the two will spend their days apart.

For nine weeks, baby cubs grow inside the female otter. She digs a special holt, hidden far away from danger, and lines it with grass and reeds. Here her cubs are born. There are two, although there could be as many as four. Tiny, blind and helpless, they stay close to their mother, drinking her milk and snuggling up to her for warmth. Their short, soft baby fur doesn't provide much protection. It will be several days before she leaves them, even for a short time, to hunt for food. Instead, her mate brings her fish.

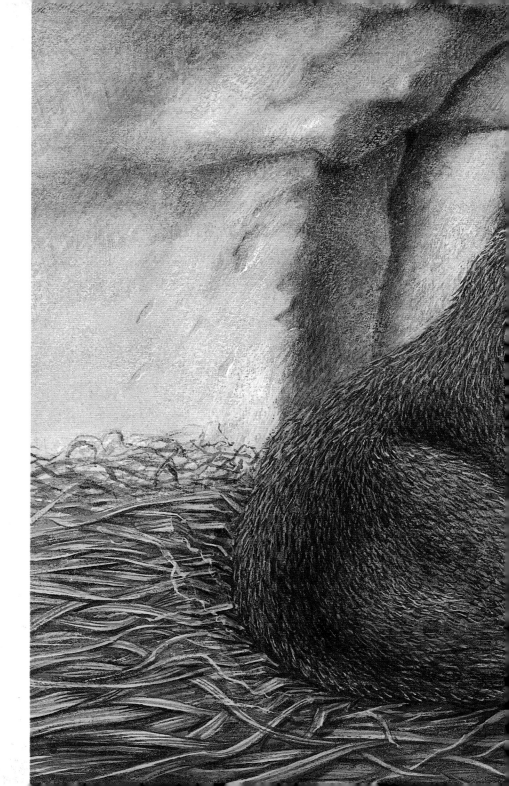

When they are a month old, the cubs' eyes open and they see the world around them for the first time. A few weeks later they take their first fumbling steps, and begin to explore. But their little legs don't always do what they want them to! They still drink their mother's milk, but she leaves them now for short periods to hunt, and brings them back pieces of half-chewed fish.

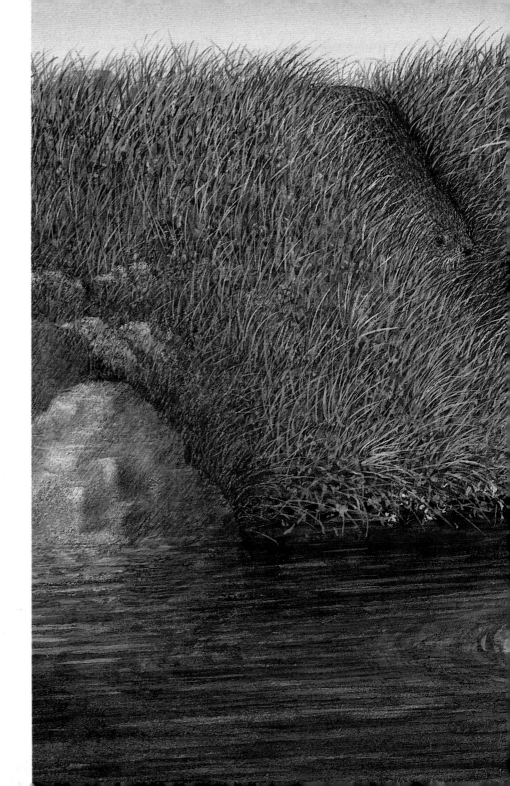

One day, when the cubs are about three months old, their mother nudges them out of the holt and introduces them to the water. The shimmering darkness is terrifying to the little otters. Timidly they watch her dive in. Then one cub glides down the river bank to join her, and the other follows. The cubs flounder around at first, but soon they are doggy-paddling along the surface.

The cubs are quickly at home in the river. One hitches a ride on her mother's back; the other swims behind her. They all have fun, playing in the water. Once they are confident, it is time to learn how to dive. Their mother takes them out to deeper water. It feels cold, and the cubs are scared. She grabs one by the scruff of his neck and pulls him under a metre or so before releasing him. Terrified, the other cub heads for the bank, but she cannot escape her turn. The cubs must dive in order to feed themselves. For their first lesson, their mother catches a small fish, and gives it to them to kill. Then she releases another fish in front of them, so they can learn how to catch it for themselves. Before long, the otter cubs will be diving and hunting on their own.

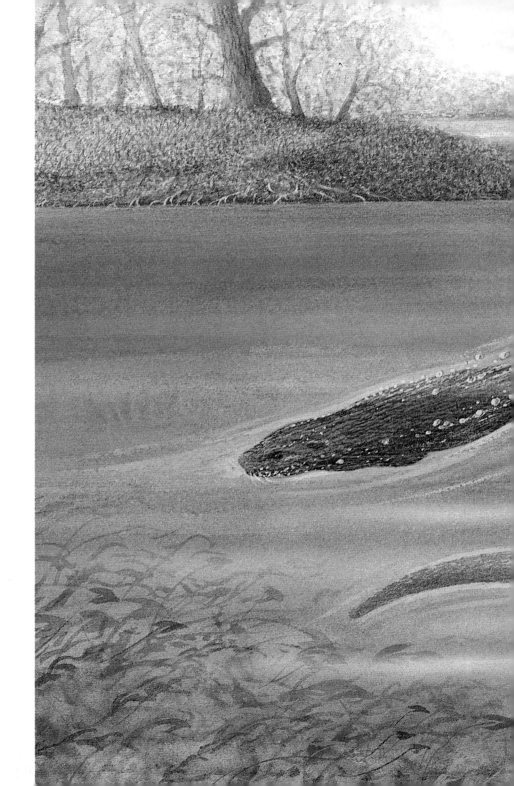

The male otter only stays with his family for a few days after the cubs are born, to bring food to his mate. Then he leaves to resume his solitary life. About a year after their birth the cubs, too, leave their mother. When they have gone she lives alone, hunting by night and sleeping by day, until the time comes when she will find another mate and bring up another family.

THE COMMON OTTER

Name: The common otter or Eurasian otter; scientific name: *Lutra lutra*.

Family: All otters are members of the animal family called *Mustelidae*, which includes stoats, weasels, polecats and pine martens.

Size: Male common otters measure up to 1.2 metres from head to tail. The females measure up to 1 metre.

Weight: Males weigh up to 11.3 kilograms. Females weigh up to 7.3 kilograms.

Distribution: Found across much of Europe and Asia. Populations have declined since the 1960s, but are increasing again in British rivers.

Habitat: Remote rivers and coastlines in wild places unlikely to be disturbed by people.

Prey: Fish, eels, frogs, shellfish; also small voles, birds and ducklings.

Nests: Called holts, usually holes in the river bank among tree roots.

Young: Usually two cubs are born, at any time of year.

Other species: The Canadian otter, which is very similar to the common otter; the giant otter of Brazil, which may be up to 2 metres long and is now very rare; the oriental small-clawed otter, which is the smallest in the world; the clawless otter; the sea otter; the smooth-coated otter; the hairy-nosed otter.

OTTER DISTRIBUTION

Otters are found on every continent except Australia and Antarctica. They were once common, but nowadays they are quite rare, because they have been hunted for their fur and to stop them taking fish. Many have also been poisoned by pesticides which find their way into rivers and then into the small fish on which the otters feed. However, in recent years the water quality of some rivers has improved, and otters are gradually making a comeback in parts of Britain.

HOW TO WATCH OTTERS

Otters are shy, elusive animals that live in remote places with few inhabitants. Look for single rocks or promontories, and check them for otter droppings, which are called spraints. Greyish in colour, these contain a lot of fish bones, and if you find any, you can be sure that there are otters around. To spot an otter, you must be prepared to wait a long time without moving, hidden behind a bank, bush or rock so you do not stand out against the skyline. Dress in dark clothes and speak only in low whispers. You may be rewarded with the sight of an otter. Do not disturb it! When you have had your fill of looking, creep quietly away.

OTTER WORDS

coat an animal's fur

cub a baby or young otter

grooming licking the fur to clean it and spread oil from the skin along the hairs

holt an otter's home, usually a hole in the river bank

hunt chase an animal for food

lithe supple and flexible

mate male or female partner

pesticide poison sprayed on crops to kill insects

prey animal killed for food

scent distinctive smell of an animal, a person or a thing

scruff of neck loose skin at the back of an animal's neck

solitary living alone

spraint an otter's droppings

web-footed having toes joined by pieces of skin, like a duck

USEFUL CONTACTS

The Otter Trust
Earsham, Bungay,
Suffolk NR35 2AF
Tel: 01986 893470

World Wildlife Fund – UK
Panda House, Weyside Park,
Godalming,
Surrey GU7 1XR
Tel: 01483 426444

Wildlife Watch,
The Green, Waterside South,
Lincoln LN5 7JR
Tel: 01522 544400

Wildlife Trust
You can check with your local library
or the telephone directory for the
address and phone number of your
local county Wildlife Trust.

INDEX

ACKNOWLEDGEMENTS

The author and publishers are grateful for the help and advice that Philip Wayre of the Otter Trust has given them in the preparation of this book, and thank Muriel Kitchen and Sergio Ransford for the photographs on the jacket.